ANG

AN INTRODUCTION

JANE STRUTHERS

Illustrations by Elena Kalistratova

summersdale

ANGELS

Copyright © Jane Struthers 2010

Illustrations by Elena Kalistratova

Cover illustration by Sarah Young

All rights reserved.

Summersdale Publishers Ltd
46 West Street
Chichester
West Sussex
PO19 1RP
UK

www.summersdale.com

Printed and bound in China

ISBN: 978-1-84953-079-8

Substantial discounts on bulk quantities of Summersdale books are available to corporations, professional associations and other organisations. For details contact Summersdale Publishers by telephone: +44 (0) 1243 771107, fax: +44 (0) 1243 786300 or email: nicky@summersdale.com.

In memory of my lovely mother-in-law,
Dorothy Martin

CONTENTS

❂ INTRODUCTION ❂

Angels are often depicted as fluffy, sweet things that float about on clouds, but actually they're formidable higher-dimensional entities who aren't afraid to use their considerable, God-given power whenever it's necessary.

What are angels? Traditional teachings tell us that they have never incarnated as humans. Instead, they come from a completely different sphere of life. Some authorities state that they were once animals, while others say they were originally elementals, such as fairies, who gradually transcended into the angelic kingdom. Yet there is a growing contemporary assumption that humans – and especially children – become angels as soon as they've died.

Regardless of what angels might be – animals, elementals or humans – they are a positive force for good and you can easily establish your own relationship with them, which will enhance your life in many different ways. This book is a simple introduction to angels, giving you some religious and historical information about them and also telling you about some of the best-known angels and the areas of life in which they can help us. The book also describes how you can work with the angels to improve your life on all levels, from increasing its spiritual meaning to helping you to search for lost objects.

❂ SECTION ONE ❂

ANGELIC LORE

This section introduces you to the role of the angels in three of the world's great religions, and also discusses the accepted hierarchy of the different types of angels.

✸ ANGELS IN RELIGION ✸

As angels are messengers of God, they play an important role in some of the major world religions, including the three great monotheistic faiths of Judaism, Christianity and Islam. However, you don't have to be religious to believe in angels.

ANGELS IN JUDAISM

The angels that appear in ancient Jewish writings were called *mal'akh* ('messenger'), *elohim* ('gods') or *bene'elim* ('sons of God'). Their roles in the oldest scriptures, including the first five books of the Old Testament, were to convey God's messages to his people, to carry out his orders and to continually praise him. They are often described in general terms as 'the angel of the Lord'.

Only two are mentioned by name: Michael and Gabriel. However, two others appear in apocryphal writings: Raphael in the Book of Tobit and Uriel in the Second Book of Esdras.

Jewish teachings eventually began to be influenced by Zoroastrianism, which was the Persian religion of the time. It spoke of a dualistic world in which good battled against evil, which was in marked contrast to the early scriptures.

The Kabbalah, which is a mystical Jewish teaching, places greater emphasis on angels. The Zohar is one of the two great books of the Kabbalah, and it describes the Tree of Life. This consists of ten intelligences (known as *sephiroth*) that are all a part of God. Each one is presided over by a specific archangel.

ANGELS IN CHRISTIANITY

Christian scripture incorporates the Old and New Testaments. Although angels appear frequently in the Bible, they are usually described as 'the angel of the Lord' rather than by name.

In the New Testament, angels are especially busy in the life of Jesus Christ, not only before his birth but also at his resurrection after the crucifixion. Luke 1:26–38 describes what happens when the angel Gabriel visits the Virgin Mary to tell her that she'll give birth to the Son of God. Later, when he's born, an angel imparts the news to shepherds in the fields, and is joined by 'a multitude of the heavenly host praising God' (Luke 2:13). Gabriel also visits Zacharias to tell him that his wife, Elizabeth, will give birth to John the Baptist (Luke 1:11–20).

Some of the descriptions of angels, especially in the Old Testament, are mind-boggling because, in human terms, they sound so bizarre. Ezekiel describes seeing angels 'of human form. Each had four faces, and each of them had four wings. Their legs were straight, and the soles of their feet were like the sole of a calf's foot; and they sparkled like burnished bronze' (Ezekiel 1:5–14). There are also strange descriptions of angels in Revelations, the final book of the New Testament, such as an angel 'clothed with a cloud: and a rainbow was upon his head and his face was as it were the sun, and his feet as pillars of fire' (Revelations 10:1).

ANGELS IN ISLAM

Islam is the third of the great monotheist religions, and was founded in Arabia in AD 622 by the Prophet Muhammad. Angels have an important role to play in the Koran, which is the Muslim holy scripture. They include the archangels Jibril and Mikhail, who also appear in Judaism and Christianity as Gabriel and Michael respectively.

Jibril plays a pivotal role in Islam as a holy messenger, dictating the words of the Koran to Muhammad and also accompanying him on the winged horse Buraq through the seven spheres to heaven. Mikhail, who is the Angel of Providence, is only mentioned once in the Koran (2:92) and has a more minor role than his Jewish and Christian counterparts.

Two other archangels appear in the Koran: Israfil (the Angel of Judgement Day), who isn't mentioned by name, and Izra'il (the Angel of Death, also known as Azrael). Both of these angels are said to be huge: Israfil's feet are said to be below the earth and his head in contact with God's throne.

There are also ranks of other angels, all of whom perform specific tasks. One rank of angels comes from heaven to fight beside Muslims in religious battles. Another holds up the throne of Allah. And angels of protection, known as *hafaza*, work tirelessly to keep demons and other evil spirits away from humans.

ANGELS AS RELIGIOUS INSPIRATION

Angels haven't only appeared in ancient religious texts bringing the word of God. From 1823 onwards, they became the inspiration for Joseph Smith Jnr to found the Church of Jesus Christ of Latter-day Saints (LDS), popularly known as the Mormons.

In LDS, angels are considered to be the spirits of humans who have already lived on earth, especially if they were 'translated' like the prophet Elijah and ascended to heaven while still alive. Some of these angels are said to be humans who have been resurrected, in which case they are especially important. Others are at a lower stage of spiritual development and act as messengers.

LDS began after Smith claimed that an angel called Moroni led him to the place near his home in the state of New York where a sacred book, written centuries before by American prophets, was buried. These writings became the Book of Mormon (it is believed that Moroni, who was a resurrected angel, was the son of Mormon) and the basis of an entire religious teaching. It's believed that when he was still a human, Moroni was the final author of what were known as the Golden Plates.

Two other Mormon scriptures – the Pearl of Great Price and the Doctrine and Covenants – also discuss angels in great detail.

✹ THE ANGELIC ✹ HIERARCHY

It is human nature to create order out of confusing ideas, so several ancient writers translated religious information about angels into something that ordinary people could comprehend. St Thomas Aquinas, who was inspired by the early writings of Pseudo-Dionysius the Areopagite, claimed that there are nine choirs of angels.

THE FIRST THREE CHOIRS

These are the choirs that surround God's throne and therefore hold the greatest power.

Seraphim guard God's throne, and are the highest angels of all. They are known as the 'burning ones' because they are alight with love and devotion to God. According to Isaiah (6:2) in the Old Testament, who saw them in a vision, 'each one had six wings; with two he covered his face, and with two he covered his feet, and with two he flew'.

Cherubim are not to be confused with the fat, winged cherubs we see in Renaissance paintings. They have a protective role and were depicted at the entrances to Ancient Assyrian temples and palaces with the large, winged bodies of animals and the faces of lions or humans. Islam texts say they continually praise God by saying 'Glory to Allah'.

Thrones are described in Ezekiel (1:13–19) as resembling humans but with four faces, and are transported on wheels covered with eyes. These strange beings are said to be angels of justice who carry out God's decisions by helping those in need and highlighting injustices.

THE SECOND THREE CHOIRS

St Thomas Aquinas wrote that these angels have dedicated themselves to spreading knowledge of God throughout the universe.

Dominions were said by Pseudo-Dionysius to regulate the angelic kingdom, although they have no need to control the Seraphim, Cherubim and Thrones because these are so close to God. Dominions manifest the mercy of God, and also bring knowledge and wisdom. Each of them carries a sceptre and a sword to show their divine power. Some writings say that the angels with power over each country on earth come from this choir.

Virtues are known as 'the shining ones', and their main duty is to create miracles. They also help humans to demonstrate courage, and they provide encouragement and help when someone is struggling with a loss of faith. According to some authorities, it was they who helped Abraham when God asked him to sacrifice his only son, Isaac (Genesis 22:9–14). They are allowed to change the physical laws of the universe when necessary, but they must also uphold these laws.

Powers are continually and fearlessly battling against the forces of evil, which include demons and the fallen angels. God has allowed them to avenge evil whenever they find it, and to maintain balance in the universe. They include the Angels of Birth and Death, and therefore they play a protective role when we enter our earthly lives and also when we leave them.

THE THIRD THREE CHOIRS
These angels have been commanded by God to take care of all humans, so they are often known as 'ministering angels'. These are the angels with whom we have the most contact. Although they belong to the final three choirs, this doesn't mean they are less important than the other angels.

Principalities are the angels assigned to protect the world's religions and their sacred sites, and some writings say they look after the world's countries as well. Principalities are also the guardians of royal families and of worldly rulers.

Archangels provide the crucial link between God and humans, because they pass on his messages to us. They are described in Jewish, Christian and Islamic texts as God's emissaries. These angels are very powerful and, led by Michael, are in control of the legions of angels that continually battle against the forces of darkness. Each of the archangels has a male and female aspect.

Angels work directly with humans to help and protect us, provided that we ask them to do so because they are not allowed to interfere with our free will. Their name is derived from the Greek *angelos*, which means 'messenger'. This choir includes the guardian angels that are assigned to each human and which stay with us throughout our lives. Angels are also the link between God and nature.

THE SEVEN HEAVENS

Seven has always been a mystical number. So, our ancestors believed that there must be seven levels of heaven as well.

The first heaven is called Shamayim, and is closest to the Earth. It is the realm of all the angels that take care of the planets, stars and the weather. It is ruled by Gabriel.

The second heaven is called Raqia, and is presided over by Raphael. The Books of Enoch, ancient Jewish writings said to have been written by Enoch, who was Noah's great-grandfather, state that it's where fallen angels and other sinners are held, awaiting the Day of Judgement.

The third heaven is known as Shehaqim. Enoch says that hell is located in its northern regions, while a beautiful paradise – possibly the Garden of Eden – lies in the south. It is ruled by Anahel.

The fourth heaven is Zebhul and is said to be the location of the heavenly Jerusalem. It is presided over by Michael.

The fifth heaven is Machon. Some of the fallen angels are said to be kept in the northern regions, while the southern regions are populated by ministering angels who continually sing God's praises. It is ruled over by Sandalphon.

The sixth heaven is Makon, ruled over by Zachiel. This is the location of the Akashic Records, which document the lives of everyone who has ever lived.

The seventh heaven is Araboth, with Cassiel as its ruler, and is the home of God as well as the Seraphim, Cherubim and Thrones.

❂ FROM MAN TO ANGEL ❂

Most people believe that angels and humans are two very different forms of life and there isn't any crossover between them. Angels can't become human and humans can't become angels. However, some religious texts beg to differ. The Church of Jesus Christ of Latter-day Saints believes that angels were once humans, and the Bible also mentions two men who had pleased God so much that they were transported to heaven and became angels.

Elijah was a Hebrew prophet who rose to heaven in spectacular fashion in a fiery chariot (2 Kings 2:11–12). Once there, it's believed that he was transformed into the angel Sandalphon, as a reward for his good work on earth. Sandalphon is said to be so tall that it would take hundreds of years to travel from his toes to his head. He acts as an intermediary who carries our prayers directly to God, so he can answer them.

Sandalphon is the twin brother of Metatron, who was also human before becoming an angel. Metatron was once Enoch, the father of Methuselah. Metatron has great power and works particularly with children, whether they're on earth or in heaven. He also helps in clearing auras of stale energy.

✸ FALLEN ANGELS ✸

Although angels are generally assumed to be benign entities, some people believe in fallen angels. These are the angels that have displeased God, often because they've gone against his orders or have tried to set themselves above him, and have been punished by being thrown out of heaven. The Powers are the angels who continually battle against these fallen angels.

Lucifer is the only fallen angel to be mentioned by name in the Bible. According to Jewish and Christian writers, Lucifer was originally head of all the angels and had great power as a result. But pride in his exalted position made Lucifer long to take God's place. When he tried to do this, he and his supporting angels were challenged by the Archangel Michael and evicted from heaven. For some writers, Lucifer is Satan. For others, there is a centuries-old confusion between the two entities.

The Book of Enoch tells of a group of angels who behaved in a way that is completely contrary to the modern view of them. These angels were so attracted to human women that they had sex with them. Their punishment was to be exiled from heaven. This is briefly mentioned in Genesis 6:2–4, which describes 'the sons of God' taking the 'daughters of men' as their wives.

❈ PAINTED ANGELS ❈

Artists, from painters to sculptors, have been depicting angels for thousands of years, although not always in a form that we easily recognise today. The Ancient Assyrians guarded the entrances of their temples by painting part-human, part-animal Cherubim on the walls. Of course, the great difficulty for most artists is that they have never seen an angel themselves, so they have to rely on their imaginations, other paintings or descriptive writings to get some idea of what an angel might look like.

Some medieval painters, such as Giotto di Bondone (c.1267–1337) and Fra Angelico (c.1400–1455), are best remembered for their beautifully detailed and richly gilded depictions of androgynous angels, all with haloes, often in a biblical setting such as the Annunciation (Gabriel telling Mary that she is going to bear a son). But not all angels looked like this. Many medieval and Baroque painters portrayed angels as *putti* – naked, chubby children with wings. These playful creatures, which were a particular favourite of Raphael (1483– 1520), were derived from Greek images of Eros, the god of love, and bore no resemblance to the angels described in religious texts.

Angels continue to fascinate artists. One of the most celebrated contemporary depictions of an angel is Anthony Gormley's massive steel sculpture, *The Angel of the North*, which towers over the A1 motorway at Gateshead in the UK.

✸ ANGELS IN THE ARTS ✸

Anyone who imagines that angels are always tranquil, celestial creatures with wings would be surprised to see Clarence Oddbody (played by Henry Travers), the 'angel, second class' who is assigned to help a desperate George Bailey (James Stewart) in the film *It's a Wonderful Life* (1947). Clarence has yet to earn his wings, although he does so in the closing moments of the film after George is reunited with his family. *It's a Wonderful Life* isn't the only film about angels, but it is one of the best-loved.

Angels frequently appear in all forms of literature, too. When John Milton wrote his epic poem *Paradise Lost*, which was published in 1667, he drew on the Book of Enoch as part of his inspiration. The poem described

29

Adam and Eve's expulsion from the Garden of Eden, and also the battle with God that was waged by Satan and other fallen angels. Two archangels – Raphael and Michael – appear in the poem. William Blake, the poet and artist, saw visions throughout his life, including that of 'a tree filled with angels'. One of his poems, 'The Angel', described how an angel dried his tears.

More recently, one of the threads in Salley Vickers' best-selling novel *Miss Garnet's Angel* concerned the story of Tobias, who travelled to Medea without realising that he was accompanied by Archangel Raphael.

✸ ANGELS IN HISTORY ✸

In recent years there have been many accounts of people's encounters with angels. It seems that the angels are working closely with us at the moment. Yet there is nothing new in this, as history tells us of several celebrated meetings between angels and humans.

JOAN OF ARC

The young woman who became known as St Joan of Arc was born in France c.1412. She was the daughter of a tenant farmer who claimed to be in contact with divine voices. What was originally one voice eventually became three – those of St Catherine of Alexandria, St Margaret of Antioch and the Archangel Michael. Other angels also communicated with her. She said they inspired her to support France in its fight with the English, who wanted to take over the crown. With the permission of the French Dauphin, Joan took part in a triumphant battle against the English at Orleans in 1429, but after more successes she was captured in 1430. She was handed over to French forces sympathetic to the English. They were suspicious of her claim to hear angelic voices and tried her on twelve charges of sorcery. The voices remained with her, and she believed that the Archangel Gabriel comforted her during her imprisonment. She was burned at the stake – the punishment for heretics – on 30 May 1431.

THE ANGEL OF MONS

There have been many stories of angels and other heavenly figures appearing to soldiers in battle. In 1415, during the battle of Agincourt between the English and French, it was claimed that the skies were filled with hundreds of heavenly archers who directed their fire at the French, who were subsequently defeated.

In August 1914, at the start of World War One, the German army was winning the Battle of Mons against the British, French and Belgian forces. The men on both sides were exhausted after days of marching, and many of them reported seeing visions of everything from castles to their long-dead mothers.

When the fighting was at its fiercest and the British feared total defeat, something very strange happened. According to the reports of several British soldiers, four or five angelic beings, with their arms outstretched, materialised between the German and British lines. At that point, the German army began to retreat. This break in the fighting allowed the British to begin their own retreat.

The story was discussed in British newspapers for months afterwards. Many soldiers and civilians involved in the war contributed their own tales, which ranged from seeing ghostly figures on horseback (the British believed they were seeing St George while the French claimed to see Joan of Arc and the Archangel Michael) to winged figures in the sky. Were these collective hallucinations or were they really evidence of the angels helping the weary soldiers?

✪ ANGELS AND MAGIC ✪

In 1583, the English magician John Dee attempted to contact angels through magic with the help of his fellow magician, Edward Kelley. Kelley would gaze into his crystal ball and the angels would communicate by spelling out words, letter by letter. This was a complicated business as the angels allegedly used their own language and alphabet. What is more, they spelled some words backwards and others in the conventional manner. The results, Dee claimed, were a new system of magic.

Although Dee and Kelley didn't use the term themselves, the language used by the angels has since been called Enochian. That is because Dee claimed that Enoch, who wrote the Book of Enoch, was the last human to have known about the language before the angels taught it to Dee and Kelley.

Dee claimed that this 'angelical language', as he called it, was used by God himself when he created the world. He also said that it was the language Adam used when he talked to God in the Garden of Eden before he and Eve ate the apple. According to Dee, Adam almost completely forgot the language after he and Eve were expelled from Paradise and began speaking in an early form of Hebrew, based on vague recollections of angelical language.

✦ SECTION TWO ✦

MEETING THE ANGELS

There are countless angels, but here is an introduction to some of the best known. In addition to the mighty archangels are your own angels, whose sole task is to take care of you from birth to death, and beyond.

✸ ARCHANGELS ✸

Archangels form the eighth choir of angels and it's their job to pass messages from God to humans. Religious texts contain many stories about them, but opinion is divided about how many archangels there are. Some sources say there are only four, whereas others claim there are nine. There are twelve archangels in the Kabbalah, and they all occupy a specific position in the ten *sephiroth* (or energetic spheres) of the Tree of Life. The Book of Revelation in the Bible states that there are seven archangels (and seven is a very significant number in Revelations), but only names Michael, Gabriel and Raphael. Who are the other four? Contemporary authors writing about angels dispense with these traditional ideas and often list many archangels.

One ancient system, which honoured the sacred significance of the four compass points, assigned one archangel to each of the four directions. Uriel ruled the north and Michael the south; Gabriel ruled the west and Raphael the east.

Such a clash of opinions adds up to great confusion, but does it really matter? Perhaps we shouldn't worry about such rankings unless we have religious or spiritual reasons for doing so. Maybe instead we should simply concentrate on the tasks performed by each archangel, so we know which one to call on when we need their help.

MICHAEL

Judaic, Christian and Islamic texts (which refer to him as Mikhail) consider Michael, whose Hebrew name means 'who is like God', to be the chief archangel. Some traditions also say that he's the head of the Virtues – the angels that help humans to show courage in the face of adversity. Michael certainly has an abundance of courage, as he is the archangel who's continually battling against Satan and the forces of evil.

Michael is often depicted holding a massive sword made from a sapphire blue flame. It's said that you often know he's near because you start to feel hot and because you see flashes of blue or purple in the air.

GABRIEL

Gabriel appears in the Christian and Jewish Bibles, and also in the Koran (as Jibril). Of all the archangels, Gabriel is the only one who's generally believed to be female. Her name means 'God is my strength' in Aramaic, and she's the angel who told Mary that she would have a child. It's said that one of Gabriel's roles is to collect each soul before birth and stay with it until it's born. As a result, she has a special affinity with children and is the angel to call on whenever you need help with conception, fertility, birth or taking care of your children. Medieval painters often showed her holding a lily, which is a symbol of purity associated with the Virgin Mary.

URIEL

Uriel, whose name means 'fire of God' in Hebrew, is one of the most powerful and important angels. Although he isn't mentioned by name, he's believed to be the angel with the flaming sword that God placed in the east of the Garden of Eden after the fall of Adam and Eve (Genesis 3:24). He's also said to have warned Noah of the impending flood. As a result, Uriel is associated with the weather (in particular, flooding, thunder and lightning), as well as alchemy and wisdom. He's an especially helpful angel if you need assistance in understanding others or in gaining an objective view of a problem.

RAPHAEL

Raphael has two important tasks. The first, for which he's probably best known, is healing, because his Hebrew name means 'God has healed'. The second is as the angel who watches over travellers, because he was the faithful (and unseen) guide of Tobias in The Book of Tobit. He showed Tobias how to make healing ointments and medicines from a fish, and therefore is often portrayed with a caduceus (an Ancient Greek or Roman herald's wand, typically with two serpents entwined around it, which is a symbol of the healing profession) in one hand and a bowl of healing balm in the other. Alternatively, he appears in his guise as the friend of travellers, carrying a pilgrim's staff. Raphael is in charge of the Powers, the choir which keeps control over the fallen angels.

❂ AN ANGELIC ❂ COMPENDIUM

These are some of the other angels who work with humans.

HANIEL

His name means 'joy of God' or 'glory of God' in Hebrew and it's said that Haniel is the head of the angelic choir of Virtues. Legend has it that Haniel is the angel who transported Enoch to heaven. It's also claimed that he protected the Virgin Mary throughout her pregnancy.

Haniel is connected with the planet Venus, which in astrological terms is the planet of love. Therefore, Haniel has a very important role to play in relationships, because he can help you to overcome any muddles or crossed wires by clearing up the confusion. He encourages clear communication between people, so that everyone knows where they stand. He's also one of the angels associated with healing, and particularly with throat conditions.

CHAMUEL

Chamuel is also known as Camuel, and his Hebrew name means 'he who sees God'. He is one of the chief angels of the Powers, who are always battling against evil, and therefore he has a very protective quality.

He's often called the angel of love because he works through our hearts. Chamuel helps us to heal all the problems, such as personality clashes, rifts, arguments and misunderstandings, that can beset a relationship. Therefore, he is the angel to call on when you need help in understanding what's happening between you and another person. Chamuel is also the angel who helps us to express ourselves through creative activities.

ZADKIEL

Zadkiel's Hebrew name means 'the righteousness of God'. It's said that he is the head of the Dominions, the angels that spread God's mercy. As a result, he's the angel of mercy, and encourages us to be generous and forgiving towards other people. If we ask for his help, Zadkiel will help us to free ourselves from negativity, limitation, narrow-mindedness, pettiness and any other thoughts or feelings that block our joy, understanding and compassion. He also helps us to be diplomatic when dealing with difficult situations or when we need to choose the right words.

Some authorities claim that Zadkiel was the angel who stopped Abraham giving his son, Isaac, to God as a sacrifice. He teaches us to trust in God's blessings, especially when life is hard.

RAGUEL

The Book of Enoch lists Raguel, whose name means 'friend of God' in Hebrew, as one of the seven archangels. It's his responsibility to ensure that the other angels are working together in a spirit of fairness and co-operation.

Raguel is the angel to call on when you feel as though you're at a disadvantage or fighting a losing battle. He'll help to boost your self-respect and motivation. He is also helpful if you're working as part of a team but you feel you aren't being given enough credit for your efforts, or if the atmosphere with your teammates has soured for some reason. He will also help you to become more organised and efficient.

JEREMIEL

Also known as Ramiel, Jeremiel's Hebrew name means 'mercy of God'. Ancient writings often describe him as being a fallen angel, perhaps because he takes care of the souls of people who've died. Jeremiel is there to greet them when they cross over, and he gives them a review of their life on earth, so they can understand what they did and didn't do.

You don't have to wait to meet Jeremiel and benefit from his help, because you can call on him to help you gain an overview of the life you're leading now. He can help you to make any necessary adjustments. He is also the angel who helps with prophetic visions and clairvoyance.

ARIEL

Ariel is often associated with lions, and in ancient times was sometimes depicted with a lion's head because his name means 'lion of God' in Hebrew. Ariel is also connected with the wind and with nature, and appears in Shakespeare's *The Tempest* in the guise of 'an airy spirit'.

Ariel is the angel to contact when you want help in dealing with nature, perhaps when you're trying to tame your garden or you want your plants to grow more healthily. He is also the angel to call on if you're concerned about the fate of wild animals – whether for environmental or conservationist reasons or because you're worried about one animal in particular.

JOPHIEL

Jophiel's name means 'beauty of God' in Hebrew, and one of his tasks is to help us to become more creative and artistic. He helps us to realise our creative potential and to come up with exciting ideas. If you have a brilliant brainwave that appears to have arrived out of the blue, it may be because Jophiel has whispered it in your ear.

Jophiel performs another important function because he's the angel of wisdom. When we call on him, he helps us in our studies and when we're preparing for exams and tests, but he also encourages us to develop the wisdom that comes from experiencing life in all its ups and downs. He encourages positive thinking, constructive ideas and an open mind.

RAZIEL

His Hebrew name means 'secrets of God' because he is said to stand close to God's throne at all times and so hears everything that God says. Tradition states that Raziel is the author of The Book of the Angel Raziel (although it's thought that it was written in the Middle Ages), which was given first to Enoch and later to Noah.

Raziel helps us to develop our innate psychic talents, whether this means tuning into our intuition on a general level or working hard at a particular skill such as clairvoyance. He also enables us to gain more insight into our lives. If your mind is usually very busy you may find it easiest to connect with Raziel through meditation or in your dreams.

✸ HOW TO KNOW WHEN ✸
AN ANGEL IS NEAR

Angels don't always appear in the way we might expect. Although they can sometimes materialise with wings or in a blaze of light, they are much more likely to manifest in less dramatic ways. Sometimes they leave calling cards, to let us know that they're near and are looking after us.

One of the classic angel calling cards is a white feather that you find in an unexpected place, rather than one that has obviously floated down from a passing bird. For instance, a feather on the lawn is most likely to have come from a bird, whereas a feather on the carpet of a room with no windows open might have come from an angel. As with any other mystical experience, you must always eliminate the obvious explanations before settling for any supernatural ones.

Sometimes angels manifest in the form of a powerful floral scent when there are no flowers or perfumes nearby. Alternatively, they may make themselves known through music (usually classical rather than rock) that no one else can hear yet, which is coming over loud and clear for you. Or you might keep seeing or hearing references to angels when you least expect them. Another typical way for angels to contact you is by appearing in your dreams. They may also appear in a way that isn't described here, but which is still significant for you.

✪ YOU AND YOUR ✪
GUARDIAN ANGEL

Everyone – regardless of who they are or what they've done – has a guardian angel. You do, too. This is a special angel who is assigned to take care of you throughout your earthly life, and who remains by your side from the moment your soul first incarnates into your body until after your death. Your angel would dearly love to help you make the most of your life, whether in important or trivial ways. Yet they can't do this unless you specifically ask for their help each time you need it, because they aren't allowed to interfere in your free will unless in exceptional circumstances.

Although your angel wants to help you, there are some things that they can't do on your behalf. For instance, they won't do anything that will harm another person in any way. And neither will they do anything that is only designed to inflate your ego, such as ensuring that everyone around you continually tells you how wonderful you are.

Asking your guardian angel for help doesn't mean that you will have a charmed life, free from trouble and anxiety. We are all given tough situations to deal with so that we can grow from the experience, and your guardian angel can't stop you having to cope with your fair share of them. But your angel can guide you and remind you that you aren't alone.

✸ ANGEL TALK ✸

How can you make contact with your guardian angel? One way is to gradually accustom yourself to the idea of this angel's continual presence, so you begin to tune into them and become more receptive to their guidance. You will find lots of exercises for making contact with angels in Section Three, but before you try them it helps to understand how angels work with us.

When you ask your angel for help, it's not enough to send out a request and then sit back and wait for everything to unfold in the way you want. You must do your bit, too. For instance, if you ask your angel to help you land the perfect job, you still need to respond to adverts, talk to people who might be able to help you or get the training you need. Your angel will be working behind the scenes but they can't do it all on their own.

Angels often communicate with us by whispering ideas into our ears. We receive these as flashes of inspiration, impulses, sudden brainwaves or moments when the penny drops, and we usually forget to give our angel the credit. Guardian angels communicate with other guardian angels too, working hard to ensure that their human charges make contact, patch up a quarrel or help one another. Don't forget to regularly thank yours for all their help!

✵ SECTION THREE ✵

WORKING WITH THE ANGELS

Being able to establish a connection with the angels will transform your life, enabling you to ask for their help, listen to their guidance and enrich your world in many other ways.

❂ CONNECTING WITH ❂
THE ANGELS

Anyone can make contact with the angels. You don't have to belong to a particular religion or spiritual group. You don't have to be an angel expert. And neither do you have to be saintly or perfect before they'll talk to you. All that's needed is to open your heart to them, and to open your mind so you're ready to receive the ideas, suggestions and guidance that they send you. You may not have realised, but angels have been sending you messages all your life. Some you may have acted on, some you may have ignored.

At first, you might feel slightly awkward or self-conscious whenever you try to connect with the angels. Your rational mind may cut in, telling you that you're being daft or that you're wasting your time because no one is there. Do your best to relax and to turn off that critical inner voice. Refuse to listen to it whenever it butts in.

It may help to listen to some beautiful music, especially if it has spiritual significance for you, because it will encourage you to relax and will put you in a receptive state of mind. Although the angels can make contact with you even when you're listening to the noisiest piece of music, you may not be able to hear them at first.

❂ ASKING FOR A SIGN ❂

If you're new to working with angels and you aren't sure if your messages and requests are getting through to them, you can always try asking them to send you a sign that they can hear you. This will reassure you that you're on the right track, and will help you to establish a stronger link with them.

However, you must be open-minded about what this sign might be without being so indiscriminate about it that you interpret the vaguest indication of angelic presence as solid confirmation.

Once you're sure that you've established a connection with the angels, you could ask them to give you some way of knowing that they're with you. You could ask them to touch you on the shoulder or to put a particular image into your mind, or find some other way of letting you know that they're near. Alternatively, you could ask them to grant a simple request. Many people like to ask to be given a parking space and this is a perfectly valid request. Angels are just as happy to help us with the mundane areas of our lives as with the bigger ones. But, each time, don't forget to say thank you!

❋ BEING WITH ❋
YOUR ANGELS

Ideally, your connection with the angels should be on a daily, or even an hourly, basis. They are with you all the time, so it makes sense for you to be in contact with them as much as possible in order to benefit from their wisdom and guidance.

Try talking to them next time you go for a walk, preferably in the countryside or a park or garden. It helps to be alone, so you can chat to them in your mind without your companion wondering why you're so silent. It's good to be in natural surroundings because watching the antics of birds and insects will help to relax you. Listen to the birdsong or the humming of bees, and feel yourself getting closer to the angels. Pay attention to the thoughts that come to you, especially if they help you to solve a problem or set aside your worries.

You can also ask the angels to watch over you while you sleep. Whenever you're ready to fall asleep, ask the angels to keep you safe. If you're anxious about something, ask them to bring you peace. Imagine one angel standing at the foot of your bed, one at the head of it, and one either side of it. Know that they'll stay with you until you wake up.

❄ CREATING AN ❄ ANGEL ALTAR

When you've begun to work with angels you might feel inspired to honour them by creating an altar to them. It can be as ornate or simple as you like, and you can have it on full display in your sitting room or tucked into a corner in your bedroom. The angels won't mind either way!

Enjoy deciding how to decorate your altar. After starting with the basics of a flat surface – which can be anything from a mantelpiece or windowsill to a table – you can let your imagination and intuition take over. If you aren't sure what to do, ask the angels to give you some suggestions and then act on the ideas that come to you.

Some options that might appeal include having some beautiful candles or tealights that you can light whenever you sit in front of your altar, but don't leave them burning unattended. You could decorate it with postcards or greetings cards showing favourite angel images, or you could design your own if you're feeling artistic. Choose a small vase for flowers or foliage, or set out some of your favourite crystals. If you want to work with a particular angel, find an image of them so you are continually reminded of their presence.

You could even begin and end each day by spending a few moments in front of your angel altar, thanking the angels for all the help and guidance they give you.

✸ DREAMING WITH ✸
THE ANGELS

One of the most effective ways for angels to contact you is in your dreams. Sometimes they'll give you a specific message and at other times you'll have a powerful dream that is so vivid it feels as though it really happened. And maybe it did, as the angels can take us into many other realms while we're asleep.

You might like to record your dreams, so you can look back at them and mull over their meanings. At first, you may only remember fragments of your dreams, but writing them down will encourage your subconscious to tell you more about them.

1. Choose a special notebook and pen with which you'll record your dreams. Don't use either of them for anything else. Keep them by your bedside.

2. Ask the angels to send you a dream that will solve a problem you're grappling with, give you a message or reunite you with a special person. Thank them, and then go to sleep.

3. When you wake, try not to move, because changing your sleeping position can make a dream vanish from your mind. Lie still, remembering as much of your dream as possible, then reach for your notebook and write down your dream in detail. As you write, you'll find that more details come to you. Thank the angels when you've finished.

❂ ASKING THE ANGELS ❂
FOR PROTECTION

Angels will always do their best to help us, including coming to our aid when we need protection. This can take any form, from watching over us while we sleep to being with us when we're in situations that make us uneasy. There are even stories of people who've been in great physical danger and have felt themselves being lifted up bodily and moved to safety – even when no one else is around. They believed that angels had helped them.

Archangel Michael is the angel to call on when you need physical protection, as he will swiftly come to your aid and bring many angelic helpers with him if necessary. No request is too trivial, so you don't have to worry about bothering him with something that you fear might be too minor for him to notice.

If you want to protect your home from the weather, such as during a violent thunderstorm, you can call on Uriel. Ask Ariel for help if you want to protect your garden or another natural environment. Summon Raphael if you need protection while you're travelling or on holiday.

Of course, even though the angels will always help you, that doesn't mean you're absolved of all personal responsibility. You must still do what you can to protect yourself by acting wisely and sensibly.

❂ PROTECTING ❂ YOUR HOME

If you're worried about your home being burgled, or you have troublesome neighbours, you'll find this exercise very effective. Practise it at night before you go to sleep, or whenever you leave your home. You can adapt it for any other situation that makes you anxious, too, by choosing the appropriate angel or asking for a suitable angel to be sent to you. It's particularly good when you park your car in a public place and want to know that it will still be there when you return.

1. Put yourself into a calm and relaxed state of mind. Take three deep breaths. Explain the situation to

Archangel Michael, either in your mind or by speaking out loud. Ask him and his fellow warrior angels to protect your home from all interference and to keep you safe, while welcoming the people you want to see.

2. Now imagine Archangel Michael standing by your front door, with his sapphire-blue sword in his hand. Know that he's guarding your home against all intruders. Imagine other angels, looking fierce and ready to attack, standing beside each window and outside every other entrance, such as your back door.

3. If you have a garden, know that a warrior angel is standing guard at each boundary.

4. Thank all the angels for their help.

✳ ASKING THE ANGELS ✳
FOR HEALING

Many angels specialise in healing, and they do what they can to encourage us to ask them for help. If we could only see them, we'd realise that tremendous numbers of angels cluster around doctors' surgeries, hospitals, clinics, hospices and other places where healing is being carried out. They are trying to create a peaceful, loving environment, but they are rarely allowed to interfere with someone's free will so there is a limit to what they can do.

But if you invite the angels to give you healing you're giving them permission to work with you, which can lead to many wonderful experiences. The first step when asking the angels for healing is to keep your thoughts positive. Healing energy will be flowing through you, so don't cloud it with doubts or negative ideas. Healing works in many ways – not only on a physical level but also spiritually and emotionally. And the one thing it always triggers is change, whether it's a change in physical health or a change of attitude.

Two of the greatest healing angels are Raphael and Haniel, and you can call on either of them to help you whether you're giving or receiving the healing. Raphael is especially skilled in healing problems connected with the eyes, while Haniel specialises in throat ailments.

❋ HEALING WITH ❋ THE ANGELS

There are two methods of giving healing: through physical contact and at a distance. Distance healing, as the latter is called, can be remarkably effective, so there's no need to worry if you're physically separated from the person you'd like to heal or the person who is healing you. Healing transcends all boundaries. This is a simple exercise for sending someone distance healing.

1. Sit comfortably with both feet on the floor. Take three deep breaths, close your eyes and mentally surround yourself with a protective bubble of white light.

2. Ask either Archangel Raphael or Haniel, the two angels of healing, to be with you. Know that they're there, even if you can't sense them.

3. Say 'Please help me to send healing to —' and give the name of the person to whom you're sending healing. Imagine them fit, healthy and happy. Put out of your mind any thoughts about the illness or any other problems that they're struggling with. Ensure that your thoughts are positive and loving.

4. If you want to send healing to someone else, imagine the first person walking away from you and the next person appearing. Repeat step 3.

5. When you feel ready to end the healing, thank the angels for helping you. Open your eyes and return fully to the room.

❊ FINDING LOST OBJECTS ❊

Y ou can consult the angels for help in dealing with major, life-changing events, and you can also call on them when you need assistance with mundane, fleeting problems. So next time you can't find your car keys or your cat goes walkabout, you can summon the angels for assistance. The angels don't discriminate between what's important and what's unimportant in the way that we do, so there's no need to worry that they'll dismiss your request as being too trivial.

When asking for their help and while waiting for your request to be granted, it's essential that you remain positive. Keep picturing yourself being reunited with whatever you've lost and feel the relief at finding it again. If you're waiting for an animal to come home, lovingly call to it in your mind over and over again. Imagine a happy reunion with your beloved animal.

Two angels in particular – Chamuel and Zadkiel – specialise in helping humans to track down things that they've lost. In addition, Chamuel gives us strength when we're worried, helping to soothe us so we can think more rationally and not descend into panic. Zadkiel helps us to rise above the sort of hopeless, doom-laden thinking that can beset us when we're anxiously searching for something. Together, they provide support and do their utmost to reunite you with whatever you've lost.

✷ ASKING FOR A ✷ SAFE RETURN

Very often, the first thing we do when we discover we've lost something is to panic. And if we can't find it after some frantic searching, we imagine that it's gone forever. Far better to summon the angels' help before we reach the point of desperation, especially as angels have the ability to see things that we can't.

1. As soon as you've lost something, get in touch with the angels. Do your best to calm down and to breathe slowly, so you become centred and better able to think properly. If you're in a public place, find somewhere private or away from other people.

2. Either say out loud, or in your mind, 'Dear angels, please help me to find —' and say what it is that you've lost. 'Please give me guidance so that I can find it again quickly.'

3. If you've lost an animal, say 'Please send — [the name of the animal] home to me'. Always thank the angels in advance for their help.

4. Pay attention to any hunches that come to you, any flashes of intuition or bursts of memory. Follow them up, all the while remaining calm, constructive and convinced that you'll find whatever it is that you've lost. Thank the angels again as soon as you find what you were looking for.

✿ ANGELS AND NATURE ✿

Our day-to-day lives are often so busy that it's easy to become disconnected from the natural world that surrounds us. Yet we're all part of nature, and this lack of connection with it can lead to many difficulties, both on an emotional and a physical level.

The Archangels Uriel and Ariel both work with nature, so you can call on them if you want to reconnect with the natural world. Ask them to help you to appreciate your natural surroundings again. If your garden is neglected, ask Ariel to help you to become enthusiastic about it. You could also call on Archangel Raguel to boost your motivation. Unfortunately, the angels won't do the digging for you, but they will call in a whole host of nature spirits to watch over your garden and they'll whisper ideas about how to take care of your crops.

Uriel also works with the weather, so he's the angel to contact if you're worried about the state of the weather coming your way. For instance, you could ask him to protect you from the worst of the rain if there's a deluge. Ariel will help you to create an organic or biodynamic garden, and he will also help you if you're involved in an environmental campaign.

✺ TAKING CARE ✺
OF NATURE

One of the most enjoyable things you can do outdoors is to grow your own food, whether that's a few herbs in a window box or an entire garden devoted to vegetables. But plants are prey to all sorts of problems, from pests and diseases to bad weather. One option is to ask the angels to help you to tend your garden. The following exercise works best if you're prepared to share some of your crops with the insect and animal life in your garden, so there's enough for everyone and everything.

1 Stand beside the plant or area of ground that you want to protect. Allow yourself to relax by taking

three deep breaths. Now tune into the angels around you.

2. If you're worried about being overheard, you can connect with the angels in your mind rather than out loud. Sit or kneel on the ground and place your hands on it. Feel the energy coming up through the earth. Feel love for the soil and for everything it provides.

3. Ask the angels to be with you to bless the land, to bless the crops and to bless all the methods you use for growing plants. Ask them to protect the crops so that you and the other creatures in your garden have plenty to eat. Thank the angels for their help.

✺ ANGELS AND ANIMALS ✺

Angels have a tremendous affinity with animals. They love working with them, partly because animals have such loving natures and partly because they don't question what they can see or feel, so they are often much more receptive to the presence of angels than humans are. Some angels have dedicated themselves to working solely with animals, while others watch over all sentient beings that need their help, from the tiniest insect to the biggest animal.

Archangel Raphael is the angel to ask for help if an animal is injured, distressed or unwell. He will be with the animal in an instant whenever you invoke his name and he'll do what he can to help. If possible, you should also help the animal in whichever way is most appropriate, which in some cases will mean summoning the vet. Animals often need medical attention as well as angelic assistance, and the angels will work with the veterinary carers to bring about the best result for the animal.

Archangel Ariel is another angel who loves working with creatures. Ariel is especially interested in helping wild animals and other forms of nature, and is the angel to summon if you're worried about the survival of a particular species or if you're concerned about conservation and the environment in general.

✪ CONTACTING AN ✪ ANIMAL'S ANGEL

Every animal has its own guardian angel, just as humans do. If you share your life with an animal you can talk to its angel whenever it's necessary. If you've already established a connection with the angel, it will be easier to ask them for help in a crisis or when you're upset. This is a good exercise for getting to know your animal's guardian angel.

1. Sit quietly, preferably with the animal beside you. Still your mind and relax by taking three deep breaths. If possible, gently place your hand on the animal. If that isn't possible for some reason, imagine that you've done so.

2. Close your eyes. Ask your animal's guardian angel to make contact with you. Be open to any ideas that come into your mind, such as an image, a sound or an emotion.

3. Politely ask the angel to tell you their name so you can summon them in an instant whenever you need them. Accept whichever name comes to you. It may be very similar to that of your animal.

4. Ask the angel to work with you in taking care of your animal, so you can keep it healthy, happy and fulfilled. Thank the angel for making contact with you.

❁ ANGELIC HELP WITH ❁ RELATIONSHIPS

We are nothing without love. And not only romantic love, but the love between friends, family, neighbours and other people we meet in the course of each day. Happy, harmonious relationships are an essential part of a fulfilled life, and the angels want us to get on well with those around us. Of course, it's only human nature for us to fall out with one another now and then, but what's important is to find ways of resolving our differences.

The angels are kept busier helping us in our relationships than in any other area of life. Three angels are particularly active: Chamuel, who's the angel of love; Haniel, who helps us to sort out communication problems; and Raguel, who encourages teamwork and fair play. Together, they do their best to smooth over little niggles and to sort out bigger clashes. However, as with all other aspects of our lives, the angels can only whisper suggestions into our ears and send us ideas. It's up to us to act on those suggestions, which often appear to us as flashes of inspiration or sudden impulses. What's more, our own guardian angel is often busy contacting other people's guardian angels so they can work together for our benefit. So much goes on behind the scenes that we aren't aware of!

✹ RESOLVING ✹
AN ARGUMENT

The angels hate us being sad, especially when we're nursing old grievances and raking over the past. They would much rather that we concentrate on the here and now, and they know how damaging it is – not only emotionally but physically too – for us to bear grudges.

Here is an exercise for contacting the Archangels Chamuel, Raguel and Haniel when you want to sort out an argument but don't know where to start.

1. Choose a time when you won't be disturbed. Sit quietly and take three deep, relaxing breaths. Tell the angels, either aloud or in your mind, about the argument. Explain to them what you

would like to happen, provided that it's for the highest good of everyone concerned. Thank them for their help.

2. Listen to their response. It may come to you immediately as an idea, a phrase that pops into your head or an image. Sometimes, however, you may feel that there is no answer. In this case, wait to see what happens.

3. Thank the angels again and ask them to continue to work with you in sorting out this problem. Be open to the thoughts that come to you, especially if they involve you being the first one to say sorry.

❈ ATTAINING ❈
YOUR GOALS

One of the best ways to achieve your goals is to keep dreaming about them. But that doesn't mean concentrating on all the hurdles you've got to jump over before you attain them. Instead, it means focusing on the finished result, when you've achieved what you set out to do and you're ready to celebrate your success.

Although you can't expect the angels to do all the work for you in attaining your goals, they can help you to attract a positive outcome by continually visualising it in your mind until reality matches your dreams. They will encourage you to keep going if you feel like giving up, and they'll give you the confidence to believe in yourself and to have faith that you'll eventually have a successful outcome.

Jophiel and Jeremiel can both help you to reach your goals. Jophiel will encourage you to think positively and he will also give you plenty of the creative inspiration that's needed to achieve your ambitions. Jeremiel is excellent at helping you to take an overview of your situation and he will also support you if you need to make major changes to your life.

❋ VISUALISING A ❋
SUCCESSFUL
OUTCOME

Keep repeating this exercise because it will help you to attract the outcome you're aiming for. However, you must also put in the physical effort that's needed to attain your goal, whether that means working away at it day by day or responding to the opportunities that arise as a result of this exercise. What you mustn't do is to worry about how to bridge the gap between the situation you're in at the moment and the final outcome. Let the angels take care of that for you.

1. Sit comfortably and take three deep breaths. Give a heartfelt smile and feel your spirits lift.

2. Now tell Jophiel and Jeremiel what you would like to happen, choosing positive language and saying that you want the outcome to be for the highest good for all concerned.

3. Visualise in detail the outcome you're hoping for. Experience all the emotions connected with attaining it as powerfully and vividly as possible, so it feels completely real.

4. Imagine the joy you're feeling being sent out into the universe.

5. Thank the angels for helping you to reach your goals. Stretch your arms and legs and slowly return your consciousness to the room.

6. Practise this exercise as often as you wish, and always believe that it will help you to attain your goals.

❂ SOME FINAL ❂
THOUGHTS...

While you slowly build up a relationship with angels, it is always wise to check that they are who they say they are. Occasionally we can encounter spirits that pretend to be something they're not, just as we can meet humans who aren't what they seem. A very simple way to test that any angelic contact is benign is to ask three times if the angel comes from God. It is a spiritual law that the third answer must always be the truth, so listen carefully to what you are told. If you're told that the spirit hasn't come from God, tell it to leave you alone in the name of God, mentally cocoon your entire body in white light and protect yourself by making the sign of the cross in the air.

✷ ACKNOWLEDGEMENTS ✷

Many thanks to Jennifer Barclay, Lucy York, Chris Turton and the rest of the team at Summersdale Publishers for their help in creating this book. I'd also like to thank my husband, Bill Martin, for his love and support. And last, but by no means least, I'd like to thank my angels for all their help in manifesting this book.